AF255809

Manifestations *of the* Singular

Manifestations *of the* Singular

One Poet's Journey
through Truth, Fear,
Love, and Death

Sam Raydān

RESOURCE *Publications* · Eugene, Oregon

MANIFESTATIONS OF THE SINGULAR
One Poet's Journey through Truth, Fear, Love, and Death

Resource Publications
An Imprint of Wipf and Stock Publishers
199 W. 8th Ave., Suite 3
Eugene, OR 97401

www.wipfandstock.com

PAPERBACK ISBN: 978-1-6667-8856-3
HARDCOVER ISBN: 978-1-6667-8857-0
EBOOK ISBN: 978-1-6667-8858-7

VERSION NUMBER 101623

Out beyond ideas of wrongdoing and rightdoing, there is a field.
I will meet you there.

—Rumi

Contents

Opening

Letter from the Therapist

Dr. Tina Rustockvsy

April 13th 1998

I met Mr. J fifteen years ago at a dinner hosted by friends when I was interning at the Boston University Health and Mental Care services assisting individuals living on the streets of Boston. It did not take me a long time to be completely overtaken by Mr. J's personality and poetic approach towards life. I instantly fell for him and the depth of the conversations we had. It is also worth mentioning what astonished me when I first met him was his ability to converse in pure modern poetry, the construction of thoughts, choice of words and the meaningful rhyming. It was all surreal. Equally, it did not take me more than that to sense a depth of delusion within him whereby, most of the time, he cannot tell what is real from what is imagined.

That aside, the chemistry and the attraction we had for one another was unshakable. It felt like I found home in this person, although I knew I could not truly be sure if I would feel the same way once I got to know the true personality behind the charming poet. I knew all the facts and that I should not engage in such an affair. Nonetheless, I did. I simply could not resist the temptation. On the contrary, I had a sense of excitement and eagerness within me to see how it may transpire. We regularly met, him and I, and it was a beautiful encounter every time. At the same time, the more I saw him the more I realized the seriousness of his illness. Eventually, I was determined to try and help him if I could.

It was a pleasant October day during one of our regular rendezvous where I confronted him with my concerns of his condition. I was surprised by the level of awareness he had and by the acceptance of the situation he was enduring. He even took the time to explain his years of coping with his delusions and how he is now at the verge of becoming completely engrossed by it. I, never in my life, met a delusional person who had no doubt about the seriousness of their condition. I felt as though I was the one being delusional. Nevertheless, it became much easier to openly talk about his condition. The poet in him was perhaps his strongest processing mechanism of all that he was experiencing. The poet personality that possessed him was a prodigy, a set of radical views on the fundamental philosophies of life - those that religions and philosophers spend a lifetime pondering. His mental state was probably the virtue of his beautiful poetry, the one that melts the heart but terrifies the mind. He told me once: "My madness is the only place I can bring home to my poetry."

With a lot of convincing and a complete submission from my end, he finally agreed to start seeing me professionally. He dictated the nature of the therapy sessions we would have. I would listen while he did most of the talking. He also chose the topics of our discussions with complete randomness instead of following my usual therapy approach. If he was to accept my offer to help him, I too must have accepted his conditions, which I did.

We continued to meet regularly outside my office. I must admit, I was astonished by how seriously he took our professional encounters, notwithstanding the fact that he paid no attention whatsoever to time. Each session would last for a few hours, and I was enjoying every minute of it. I was constantly thinking about him when I was with other patients and with excitement I was always looking forward to our next session. One day, as I was eagerly awaiting our fifth professional encounter at the usual five o'clock timing, he did not show up. Weeks, months, and years passed, and I did not hear from him. He had disappeared.

It has been fifteen years since we first met each other, and it still aches every time I think of him; I miss our encounters. Somehow, I also grew to admire him more in his absence, no matter how hard I tried to let go of my feelings. I was going through a real and intense experience of loss.

I finally realized that I could not continue living like that. I was hanging onto the hopeless idea of him showing up at my doorstep one afternoon. I became delusional myself, to say the least, clinging to a sweet encounter of the past that grew with time to possess my entire being. It was time for me to help myself move on.

The answer came in the form of this book. What if I could collate all the encounters we had, the discussions, and the poetry he told into a book. If I could do that, perhaps I could contain my emotional thoughts of him into such a project, and then I could finally find the closure I was looking for.

It took considerable time and effort to put this book together. It helped that he wrote his poems on napkins, and that I kept each one until today. Also, it was a process for me to go back in time and remember our conversations, capture their essence, and restructure them along with the poems into four chapters that eventually produced this book. I certainly would like to think that I did my best to truly portray the poet in him with this book.

Finally, this book may truly open new perspectives for the readers. Although you may find some of its content dark and radical in its manifestations, take it in with an open mind. Like Horace once said: "He is either a madman or a poet", and in this book you have both.

Yours Sincerely,
Dr. Tina Rustockvsy
Psy.D, PhD in Psychological and Behavioral Science

Chapter 1

Truth is a Journey You Only Seek Elsewhere

First Encounter

We are truly born with the first memory we hold.

What happens before is just life. Life being formed.

There is a margin of insanity in everything that follows.

The life we think we know and the one we end up living.

Fictional subsistence.

Not everyone can understand it. Poets perhaps.

Life in this form is not meant to be lived by everyone.

Social creatures are herds of different kinds blind folded by self-preservation.

To look for more is an inner calling. To find more is to look within yourself.

The one unique self that is carrying the essence of your being.

There can be no portion in what you seek.

It is everything or nothing.

I am only saying this because my soul is merely a manifestation of the shadow of my thoughts.

Sometimes I crave for an illusion in my reality.

Sometimes I only think of my reality as an illusion.

And at times when I doubt my existence,

I desire that illusion for a moment.

No matter how real or unreal it is.

It is pitiful. Perhaps confusing too.

If I had the choice, I would rather live in an endless sphere of silent existence.

Like an empty pool in an abandoned school.

I envy the deaf for they have one voice to listen to.

If only I could live this way.

But life by all its measures keeps throwing stone-shaped thoughts at me.

Thoughts screaming words and words looking for meanings.

Those that only exist in places you would least expect.

Then living becomes a necessary burden.

A sequence of random coexistence, swaying between logic and inflicted contradiction.

To wake up from one dream, to start another, or even to live in one.

Mine is a life lived in layers of multiple dimensions.

So dimensional that I always drift.

I travel in a space of my own wicked thoughts.

Blackholes of my own if you will.

You see,

I spend my everyday life living while my mind spends every minute questioning why.

Maybe what I am in search for is not there to be found.

Maybe I am just a troubled fool controlled by self-inclined views.

Perhaps it is truth I seek. Perhaps ultimate truth is my only path to seek.

The one that makes sense of it all.

The truth that liberates me from my very own existence.

Inward Occupation

I am craving a new reality

One that involves no humanity

No kind of establishment

Love or attachment

Territories or identity

An incognito of space and capacity

I am craving a new reality

One without a society

No boundaries nor identities

No time or memories

Just mass, motion, and profanity

I am craving a new reality

Where life is about infidelity

Where god is nature

Religion is love making

And the future is changing

A new reality

That starts with infinity

And ends with possibilities

An encounter

Free from sanity

No dot of profit

No king or prophet

Just souls surfacing ...

An inward occupation

For will and ability.

Ticking Clock

I am a demon

One that erased any sense of belonging

In my singularity I find peace

Way above all the creatures of time

Sometimes I fly high and sometimes I sink deep

In my isolation

I am connected to all what is real

Away from collective wisdom

This earth seems to believe

What humanity has taught me

Is not to feel

For,

There is only greed

Weighing up high and beneath

The perpetual flux of being

Is nothing but human's eagerness to feed

Souls made of steel

And brains washed away by a small breeze

An imaginary life they all seek

Fantasies of fullness

About peace and green

In my isolation

I saw humans stuck in a bowl

Chasing a ticking clock

Admiring a reincarnated stupidity

Of what they think or believe

About making life and creating dreams

I saw castles built

Children born

Rich fighting the poor

And poor seeking the rich

Love being made

And kids play

I saw people fight and kill

For causes they think exist

And then I saw religion justify

"This is all for the gods"

Promises for the weak

False hopes to seek

True lies spoken by priests

Loud mouths, big ears

All preaching

What life is supposed to be

Then in my isolation

I cracked open a small window

And invited all that I saw

I wanted to share what is it like to live real

And before I knew it

I looked up to see

A shadow of a big bowl

Surrounding me

In panic I ran towards the small window

But alas to no escape,

Rather walls all around me

I stood, and my isolation has gone,

All that I can hear

Is a ticking clock

… and I started to run.

No Wise No Fool

Life speaks to me in an unhinged voice
One can separate from thy' own
For all pursue validation for existence
From sin of self, mankind seeks freedom

One is intelligent, one ought to know better
The mind is deceptive and full of perception
The journey to salvation is eternal solitude
A singular path one must follow

From known roads man can learn no more
Only by letting go of who you are
Reins of the mind fly and'
In an unhinged voice life then speaks

No wise, no fool, just naked truth.

Chapter 2

Fear is to Sometimes Live
with Your Own Thoughts

Second Encounter

Think of the few emotions that can shake you up sometimes.

Do not examine why they do so.

Just observe their state of rawness and you will understand.

They may not be real to the outside world, but they certainly are to you.

You live with them.

Just because you live with them on your own,

does not necessarily mean they are not true.

This state is the vertex of reality.

A primal emotion that has the power to protect and destroy at the same time.

That chill that creeps up on your entire being and internally builds up to the point of breakdown.

You can fool yourself into believing otherwise but deep down you know it.

When the time comes, you are dancing around fire.

The chill never really goes away.

You face what terrifies you, but it is far more than that.

It is an existential part of who you are or who you have become.

The idea of living with the past is life stuck in a time capsule.

You must deal with that present and permanent state every day.

All the surprises it brings along.

Children are the bravest because their fears are still developing.

Sometimes, what keeps you awake at night are not things you are afraid of.

They are the shadows you grew up with that never left you.

They are as alive as you are.

You may live with your fears, but you can never doubt how real they are to you.

Fear of the Night

All my fears visit me at night
When I am about to give in to dreams
But my sleep never falls asleep
Awake it keeps me
In long nights of dark solitude

I think about the world
The life I am enduring
The what ifs and all what is wrong
Like an engine my mind roars
Chasing a past I want to avoid
An occasional thought of relief
Is what I hang on to
In those long moments of insomniac gestion

Then another dawn falls upon me
Like a child I await sunrise
Excited, I am a knight,
Who won a battle against the night
I have not slept in a lifetime
But victorious I stand in the morning,
For I survived
Another night against my mind

During the day

My fears fear me

But at night

Again, they reappear

At first, I avoid them in patience

Slowly they crawl in as darkness falls

I sip my drink with an occasional sleeping pill

I am tired after a long day

And so, I await my rest

But anxious I become the longer I wait

Because at midnight

Another life of mine begins

My mind suddenly awakes

Like an alarm bell hitting the clock

A memory lane

My thoughts create

From childhood until today

I go back in time

Unwelcomed visitor to my past

All the pain

I live again

In silent screams

I run

Chasing holograms

Confronting demons

Alive'

In a field of buried emotions

I become'

Chapters of my past

I vowed not to visit again

But past midnight

I am living another life of mine

Finally, my tiredness sways in

With a beaten body I lay

Awake in bed staring at time

Then dawn whispers again

Announcing the rise of a new sun

I bow and thank god

I am a creature of the night

Who survives to see daylight.

Looking War in the Eye

When I was a child
I looked war in the eye
And you know,
Nothing is more sincere than'
A child's honest eyes

Grownups back then
Were too busy killing each other
The old, the elderly,
Were too busy running away
Only children had enough fear in them
To look war in the eye
And wonder'
What is war all about
What horrible business that is
Making my family die

Now that I am a grown up
I realize why man looks man in the eye'
Merely, a common courtesy
Acknowledging mutual deceit
For,
Nothing compares to how illusory

The manhood cycle is

Eventually,

The innocent die while cowards' rule

The reasonable few are the remaining fools

And the thing about history is'

Well, what everybody knows

Not that I could change anything

When I reflect and look back

It is, nonetheless, very clear to me now

War in this jungle of life on earth

Would stand no chance

If it were not for grownup men like me.

Cheating Death

How does it feel right?
When there is only hunger outside
Out on the doorstep
There is a monster looking for bread
To feed the dead,
Those living in your head

How does it feel right?
When life's suffering meets no end
When you grow up looking for an end
Enduring an endless demeanor
A numb state of being
Living not to forgive nor forget

Just as the doorbell rang
You have made your choice
Not to regret, rather neglect
All the sympathy that brought you ahead
Chopping your breakfast
On your favorite mirror deck
Looking into your own eyes
With every sniff (that is) blowing off your head
Remembering what it is like
To live your life cheating death.

Chapter 3

Love is Not the Light in the Fire

Third Encounter

Let me tell you a story.

Love is not about passion and glory.

Tales of love are hideous and foolish. Love is not permanent.

A night you lost your mind. Lust, purity, flame and serenity.

Random variations of the heart.

I only loved what I lost in my life.

Loss is perhaps what makes love so worth having.

I am not a man of great ability to hold on to what feels right for long.

"Things between us feel different now
The bubble we lived in, it burst.
We have changed, you and I,
The spark we once had is no more.
I still think of you though,
Perhaps not every day,
Between my mind and soul
Sometimes I find you there."

I personally chose wine to resemble my drink of love.

Wine is so content in its own environment.

The first sip from a corked bottle tastes like no other. So is newly discovered love.

The rest of the bottle is really time passing.

"Every time I see you

I have a drink in my hand

Have you ever wondered

Every time I missed you

It is the drink

I am so longing for!"

It is said that the real form of love is love being made. Perhaps not.

Those rare moments where mind, soul and body are in tandem.

"Inches of lust

Miles of trust

This is how love is made"

In the end, poets are always seeking what is not there.

Love is not meant to be understood.

Love is parts unknown and parts untold.

Foolish at First

I met you at school
Now,
I am quarter of a century old
Yet,
I still cannot get over you
You,
Survived all my memories
The vanished and the new

I still remember the first time I saw you
How we instantly fell for each other
Although I knew, right at that moment,
This would be too good
To last and be true,
But little I cared back then
For all it mattered
My teenage life meant nothing
If I cannot have you
The way I was drawn to you
Every recess of every day
Time stood still
I hated weekends
For,

It kept me waiting

Until the next time I will see you

I still remember

The first smile you threw at me

The soft lips and the deadly looks

Made my day, every day,

The courage I built up

Just to approach you,

The times I rehearsed in my head

The first words I would say to you

And how easy it was

To just be myself

When I spoke with you

You made me grow up so fast,

I saw my future before me

How I would age desiring you

I had no plans back then

Besides stealing time from you,

Convincing myself was the hardest

"This is a dream, the longest I will ever have"

And how true it was

The time we spent together

Is now all I have left

Like a fictious scene

From a fairytale play

You have moved on

And I am still hanging in there …

Years passed and you still found your way

To always live between my thoughts

Not a single day pass

Without a visit from you

Like a distant memory

I watch you

All the people I have been with

All the times I fell in love

I now realize

This was just me

Collecting pieces of you.

Prey

Just like a prey
On a sunny day
I am the hunter
And she is running away

Playful fools
In a vast world
I am ready for the catch
And she risks being there

Time lapses but'
It is not like we care
Out on the edge
We have always played
Flirting with ideas
Condemned with desire
We live by the hour
As it comes at best

"Cause I got the troublesome
And she is magic made
She sparks a moment
Every time I lay my eyes on her"

She appears like June
On a winter's day
Takes the sun
And fades away

Like a predator
losing sight to prey
Every time I am close
She slips away…
She has got the rhythm
I got the base and'
To chase in vain
Then losing her
by winning this game

Life is brief
And not meant to stay
I know … I
Run for it everyday
Like a hungry morning
Starving for the day
I keep the chase
She always escapes

Foolish we play

Trapped in a way

But we both know

It is worth it that way …

31

"Cause I got the troublesome

And she's magic made

She sparks a moment

Every time I lay my eyes on her."

The Lady of the Ironclad

The lady of the ironclad

Courts her men in a cage

Silk bars all around

Candles and mirrors alike

Threads of thought guard her

The ones fine wine prays for

Inside her cage a festival break

Every time she calls for

A ritual of shameless desires

Music, liquor, and erotic flames

In secret haven at night

Her morphing starts

A celebration of lust she demands

Master to her objects inside

The night lives long

Like a thousand in one

Finally, when dawn sets for the day

An innocent creature she returns

Absent to the human eye

Only to a few she unveils

She is the lady of the ironclad ...

She runs with a plan

Far beyond any man's

Not like any

She can love many

Draws her life

Like a hammer to the skull

Once with a lover

Another with a friend

Her sexual desires

Are hers to own

She may never come

But her men always do

Her body is made

To satisfy countless but not her own

None can give it all

Plenty can barely cope

She plays between smiles

Deadly as her charm

Her mind is set to take

From those who do not give

Lucky are the men who

Get locked in her cage

For, she is the lady of the ironclad ...

Chapter 4

Death is a Master of Disguise
with All Colors of Life Combined

Fourth Encounter

Sometimes it is alright to start your story by writing the ending first.

This is an important subject to me.

I have seen death during my birth. It did not scare me.

Death is glorified in ceremonies and rituals.

Romanticizing those who cannot hurt us anymore.

We hang their pictures after they die. We even name streets after them.

Do not be fooled.

Only mothers can mourn the loss of a child.

The rest mourn to forget.

Human's selfishness sermonized the death they could not understand.

Glorified it in stories about fire and heavens.

Recitals sang in temples and churches.

Hypocrites to the clowns.

Death is no tragedy.

No passage no stairway.

Death could be a wish sometimes.

There is no more when there is no one left.

What really remains are those shadows that live with the living, until they are not.

Redemption

I found my redemption in a place far away
I have come a long way to witness my end
The glory I once had
Drove me to my finish line

I have been unfair' and
I know it is too late now
The guilt I feel
Eats at me for the rest of my days

I have come from far
To wash the sins that weigh upon my soul
Not seeking forgiveness rather remedy
From a chronicle face of an aging man

I would break all promises
To be the child I once was
I now hold my sighs until the day I die
Where I see myself nestled among your bosom's embrace

Maybe in my infinite end

I will come across you once again

So, would you hold my heart in your soft hands

And leave my last breath to fade away

37

Between the mountains and by your side

I will repeat your prayers

Maybe my wish comes true

And we meet once again.

In My Mind

In my mind
I got places to find
Hidden in layers
of psychopathic lies

I hear this voice
Rumbling, creeping
Deep inside
My self-righteous high
I have come a long way
In my solitude time
And when death finds me
I will be far gone

Fearful strength visits me
Time after time
Fighting
Not to survive
Somehow in my mind
I always tend to dive
Deeper in search
For any signs of life
It is not being that I repel

It is in mindful thoughts

Where living really starts

When we depart

~ In consciousness I float

Becoming myself as one

Leaving this earth is nothing after all ~

So, lord make the sky

Rain in prayers and gold

Because when I choose to go

I will be scratching at life's door.

Torn

I am torn

Down to my core

My world no longer rotates

Everything around

Is in static shapes

The selfishness I have

Is not a burden anymore

I am free

Free from reason'

Laws of the land

Do not bound me anymore

I ceased to be your equal

I want to play god and end you

You kings and clowns

All your sins

Your daughters and kins

And your empty hearts

You cannot hurt me anymore

Look deep down my soul

And you will find a hole

That can fit you all

All of what remains of you

Your madness and hardships you left behind

The generations you plowed

With your hatred and rorts

I will bury it all

Deep down my torn soul

And let it burn to flames

If only I could.

Closing

Loss of Separation

Am I alone in this world?

A visitor

Like a stranger in a room

There is action all around me

But for some reason

I do not belong

Time passes me by

And I watch it slip through

No sense of community, drive, or purpose

Just a strange feeling

Constantly reminding me

How cognitively lifeless

I am from the inside

That smile on my face

Do not be fooled

It is only a celebration

Of my everlasting funeral

Commencing

Dancing in joy

And burning inside my soul ...

Life goes on

And I watch

The sad comfort

I always relate to

How can I still breathe and be around?

But nothing to look forward to

Like a number that adds to nothing

Neither odd nor even

A ticking clock

Running voices in my head

Over and over again

Assuring me

This is the life to expect

… Years passed and nothing to look back to

What remains

Old memories haunting me

I sail away

In an empty vessel

Lost in a dark sea

Calm and quiet

Heavy

Sinking

Peacefully watching the end coming near

Yet, no sense of fear or relief

Just that same feeling

I am dead but I can still breathe.

www.ingramcontent.com/pod-product-compliance
Lightning Source LLC
Chambersburg PA
CBHW070735030726
47601CB00001B/24